D1030639

9780812904598

ON AND OFF THE STREET

ON AND OFF THE STREET

Bob Adelman
and
Susan Hall

Photographs
by
Bob Adelman

The Viking Press
New York

First Edition

Jacket and text design by Ira Friedlander and William Hopkins

Copyright © 1970 by Bob Adelman and Susan Hall

First published in 1970 by The Viking Press, Inc.
625 Madison Avenue, New York, N.Y. 10022

Published simultaneously in Canada by
The Macmillan Company of Canada Limited

Trade 670–52411–5   VLB 670–52412–3

Library of Congress catalog card number: 79–123016

Pic Bk 301.1   1. Urban life
2. Racial relationships

Printed in U.S.A.

1   2   3   4   5   74   73   72   71   70

Authors' Note

This is a true story—photographed and recorded as it happened.

We found Vincent and Danny walking arm in arm down a street. They told us they'd been off-and-on friends for years, and that they liked to do things together. They became our friends, too, and during a two-month period we spent many afternoons "keeping up" with them, photographing and recording whatever they happened to do and say. We didn't coach; we just tailed them, and discovered that their adventures, which seemed random and purposeless, were actually structured by the boys' relationship. This book is a distillation of that portion of their lives we were privileged to share.

—Bob Adelman and Susan Hall

Vincent and Danny
are friends.
They live in New York City
in a neighborhood
west of Central Park.
The streets are their playground.

"That's all I have. One skate. All you have to do is learn to balance with one skate."

"That's not going to work, Vincent. I'll walk and you lean on me."

"What happens if you become a pole and I go around?
Going round like a merry-go-round!"

"My head gets dizzy."

"My feet are killing me. I feel like taking the skate off, but my baby sister has my shoe. I told her to hold it for me. I'm sorry, Danny, but I've got to get a shoe."

"Let's walk through Broadway to your house."

"Hey, Danny, there's a guy in a box. He's locked in there. You don't believe me, come over here and see."

"He's locked in there, O.K. Let's get that jack-in-the-box."

"Give it back to the boy, Danny. You stupid, you can't take his box. I'm going to bite you off."

"I dare you, and I'll knock your brains out. Come on in."

"I'll hold the box and you get in."

"Come on, Vinnie."

"It's like someone's after you. You're running and you're hidden. It's like you have a broken leg."

"Come on, Vincent. March."

"This box reminds me of a refrigerator box."

"It's like you're in an Army tank."

"When we stole the box from that guy, it's like war."

"We could have a war in this box. But the enemy could stick his big hand right through that hole."

"When some soldier walks in to look for you, you hide."

"Like a tank. I could stick my fist out there and punch somebody. I'd like to be mailed to New Hampshire, Vincent."

"Acapulco."

"It doesn't exist."

"It does so. I looked on the map. It said Mexico City, and then I looked down and it said Acapulco. It's a good name, so I think it would be a good place. They got a lot of hamsters there."

"If I'm mailed, you'll have to put my zip code. Vinnie, let's turn around."

"Wait. I got me a hole. It's warm in here."

"Don't turn the box around. Turn yourself around."

"I'll turn you around. You feel like a robot. I walk like a robot. Stiff. Straight legs."

"Like a tank."

"I get embarrassed walking down the street.
I feel like laughing real hard."

"That other guy was scared of us, I don't care how big he is."

"I think he was four feet six. He was scared of us.
But if we were just one, maybe he would still run away."

"He's scared of black people, maybe."

"He thinks we're pretty strong. I am. And you will do anything."

"We messed up that box."

"Danny, put it forward.
Can't you do this?"

"That board had a staple in it, Vincent. It was sharp."

"Yes, it has a staple. It scratched me too. It hurt.
I didn't do it on purpose. No."

"Don't say 'No.' You were hitting me with that board."

"I was trying to hit the board in your hand.
I wasn't trying to hit you on your face or nowhere
where it would hurt."

"So you could get me, right?"

"No. . . ."

"Man, you were going after me."

"I know. But first I was trying to get the board off your hand.
Then when it hit you, it hurt.
By mistake, I think. It could have hit you bad.
Oh, I wonder how I got that?"

"What?"

"This scratch."

"You had that all the time, or you scratched yourself. Stop lying."

"I'm sorry I hit you."

"You hit me."

"I'm sorry. I said I'm sorry. I didn't mean to do it.
When you dropped the board and ran over here,
I thought you were faking."

"You hit my hand. Don't think I'm faking."

"You know you could have hit me somewhere,
'cause those boards were loose.
Shake hands."

"You can't shake my hand. You ain't touching this hand."

"O.K., I'll shake *my* hand."

"Let's go to Castle Lake, Vincent."

"You know the kites in Castle Lake, they go 'way up in the sky. You can't see them sometimes."

"Let's go to Castle Lake."

"I got a secret way to go. You know how to climb?"

"What do we have to climb?"

"The wall."

"That's easy."

"Not the one we're going to climb. I'm taking the real way. The new way."

"I'm bigger than the Empire State Building."

"You're a monstrosity. Look at the prickers. Look out. They're going to stick on you, baby. Come on, Danny. You've got to be careful of them."

"How do you put this on, Danny?"

"I'll do it for you. Are you a beginner? Are you good at flying kites?"

"Yeah."

"If you're so good, I'm going to put the string on expert.
I have one at home and I know how to work this."

"I'm not so good."

"Let the string go. Put it on the ground."

"Wait, stupid! You're crazy, Danny."

"No, I'm not."

"You're not supposed to let the whole roll go."

"Wait. Let me wind it for a minute."

"You can't even fly it."

"I see Castle Lake over there."

"I know you do. Danny, I'm going to hit you. Hurry up.
Can't you wind it up any faster?"

"Stop falling on the ground. You're a bird and you can't even fly.
This never goes up in the sky. Always comes down. Darn it.
I'm going to straighten it out. Oh, man, it keeps on flipping over.
Come on, bird."

"I might just take off my shoes and go in the lake, Vincent.
They'll let you go in."

"They won't. Only dogs, baby. Only dogs."

"You're barking like a dog. *Woof, woof.*"

"You're acting like a dog. You want to be a dog now.
I wish I was magic. I wish I could change into anything.
First I'd change into a snapping fish, so you could catch me."

"I'd turn into . . . let me see. What should I turn into?
Oh, I'd turn into a manta, and I'd start swimming."

"A what?"

"A manta. A fat, flat fish."

"I'll turn into a teeny-weeny baby whale."

"Roll up your shoes, Vincent. I mean your pants."

"Don't you see that bee coming over here?"

"Where?"

"You see a bee coming after you, and you don't take off your shirt."

"I'm going to step in there with my complete foot. Do you want to?"

"No."

"Come on in, Vinnie."

"I'm going over here. It's my best spot. It's deeper over here, baby."

"When I touch this rock right here, I slip. It's cold."

"It's cold. Burn-up cold."

"Get in with both feet like I did."

"At the same time?"

"Yeah."

"You could slip off that rock, man."

"I did it. Right?"

"I know. But you could slip off that rock."

"Do it. Do it."

"I could jump, but. . . ."

"Do it. Just walk in."

"Walk in?"

"Do it. Put one foot over there, then the other foot."

"You could slip off that thing."

"I could stay in here all day."

"You push me in and I'm going to knock you out."

"Now you do it, Vinnie."

"What?"

"Stand on both feet on that rock."

"What rock?"

"What rock!"

"I don't trust you. I'm scared."

"I trusted you. I'll stand over here. Go ahead."

"I don't trust you, Danny. Get over there."

"You were right in back of me, man, when I got in.
I didn't trust you either. But then you didn't push me in. So . . .
I won't push you in."

"Let's walk out to those big rocks, Danny.
You keep on walking and I'll be there. O.K.?"

"You come."

"O.K. I'm coming. Hurry up. I'm coming. Now I'm getting in.
Oh, I'm going to slip."

"Come on, Vincent."

"Hey, look, Danny!"

"So. . . ."

"Now I got in. Now I'm a big shot."

"Oh, come on, Vinnie."

"Let's play tag."

"I'll choose you for it.

Engine, engine, number nine,
Going down the track so fine.
If the train goes off the track,
Will you get your money back?"

"Yes."

"Y-E-S spells yes, and out you go.
You're out.
You said whoever is out, is it."

"But you have to get both feet
out."

"You cheat."

"Let's play follow-the-leader.
Leader."

"Second leader."

"Look at that goldfish, Vinnie, right beside this stick."

"It's not there. Oh, I wish I was magic. I'd turn into a goldfish, then I'd turn into a sea monster and get one of those fish."

"I'd get me a stick."

"I'd turn into a net, then I'd take myself a *whooop* and then I'd fly like a bird, then I'd drop down to the fish and make a *ping* and carry it home."

"See, it's still there."

"No, I wouldn't go through all that problem. I'd just go *ping*, *ping* right here."

"Have you found the kite?"

"What kite? Oh, my kite."

"You better look for it."

"You ain't going down there, Danny."

"Yeah, I am."

"You gotta climb a fence to get out of here."

"I'm going down there."

"Are you good at climbing a fence like this? You ready?"

"I ain't going to go climbing. I'm going back over the rocks. That will be much easier."

"Come on, Vinnie."

"Oh, baby. You better keep cool."

"Let's go roofing, Vincent."

"Roofing?"

"Going on roofs."

"You crazy? Step one inch of my roof and the super will come."

"In my building I can go up on the roof."

"I can go up on the roof here, but they won't let me. You have to sneak up. Come on, Danny."

"Where?"

"The roof."

"We can run around, Vinnie."

"Guess what you can do? Go up on the roof and go down the whatchamacallit up there . . . the fire escape, and then we can jump down."

"Oh, yeah, let's sneak up."

"I'm going down the fire escape, Danny."

"What's the point of doing that?"

"You can go down the ladder and keep going to the bottom. I used to do it. I'm scared now."

"I could get up that roof ledge easy, Vincent."

"Want to go down, Danny?"

"What?"

"Want to go down?"

"Do I look like it? I don't want to. Let's throw some water down there."

"Not over there. The super's over there."

"It's hard to get up this slope."

"Danny, you almost hit that lady."

"What?"

"You almost hit that lady."

"Did I? Here are some old pajamas. I'm going to throw them down."

"If you throw them down, I'm getting out of here."

"I'd say that person was lucky. You see those pajamas hanging on the rail. You see them?"

"If the super comes up here, Danny, I feel sorry for you. I'm going to say you're the one doing it."

"I feel sorry for you, Vinnie. If he comes up here I feel sorry for you. Because it's your building, not mine."

"Danny, you see that glove I threw down. That kid, he thought it was a hand."

"You see that can top down there, Vinnie? I threw it."

"Liar."

"I did."

"Who did it hit?"

"Nobody. I went *yaaa*. It splashed water all over."

"We goin' all the way down?"

"All the way. O.K. Watch your feet, Danny. It's slippery."

"Here I go, Vinnie. The first one is quite dangerous. If you fall back, it's the end of you."

Vincent: Doggie, doggie, doggie,
        step right out.

Danny: I'm on your side, Vincent.

Vincent: No, last one who's out, I got.
        I hope Ivan's on my team
        'cause I know he's good.
        Doggie, doggie, doggie,
        step right out.

Ivan: I'm on your side, Vincent.

Vincent: We're up.

Danny: How do you know?
        We've got to choose for ups.
        You and me, Vincent.
        I've got odds.

Vincent: Evens. This is evens. We win.

Mark: You gotta shoot three times.
        You're cheating.

Vincent: O.K. One. Two. Three. Shoot.

Mark: Danny and me are up first.
        We won.

Vincent: What are you doing, Danny? You've got to hit off this step.

Danny: What?

Vincent: Stupid. Hit off the step!

Mark: We'll lose anyway, Danny.

Danny: Yeah, I know. We'll lose 'cause he's got Ivan.

Vincent: So. Two against two. Get over there, Danny. You started off. You gotta accept it. Now shut your mouth.

Mark: We gotta have a good man.

Vincent: Here's a home run. Here I go, baby.

Mark: You're out, Vincent. Ivan's turn.

Vincent: You're crazy. I gotta get my turn.

Mark: Then how come you strike? You're cheating.

Vincent: O.K. Here, Ivan. But we're going to get a long time up.

Vincent: Home run. We won, Ivan.

Mark: But you had Ivan on your team. He's a good player.
You had two good players on your team.
We had two bad players on our team. Right?
Right? Right?

Vincent: O.K. We'll switch.

Ivan: Me and Mark against you and Danny.
Mark, come here.

Vincent: You two guys are good, and Danny's bad.

Ivan: Danny's good. Mark ain't so good.

Vincent: You two are better than us. It'll be slaughter every time.

Mark: Maybe we're better, but you're good, Vincent.
So why not me and Ivan or me and you?

Vincent: See, I'll prove it to you. That Danny ain't good.
It'll be slaughter every time.

Danny: Wait, Vincent. I quit. I quit.

"You going to play or not, Danny?"

"I ain't playing. Those kids made me look like a bum player. They're good players."

"Hey, Danny, come on."

"I don't want you, Vincent. I don't want nobody."

"Well, that means you don't want to play?"

"You're not going to convince me. It's unfair."

"I know it's unfair. It would be slaughter. Tell me how we're being unfair to you."

"You're such good players. That's why."

"What makes it unfair?"

"I don't practice at all."

"Danny, you want to play, or not? One more time. Yes or no? Are you going to play?"

"No."

"What's the use of talking when you ain't going to do a thing? I ain't going to talk to you about nothing."

"I ain't talking to you, you snotty brat."

"I talk to you, but you ain't listening to me."

"I listen to my mother, but not you."

"Your mother! Come on, Danny. You're not going to be on my team?"

"I won't do it. I won't play or listen. Not even if you give me a million dollars. A billion, maybe. For a billion I'd join your team for a second. But not for a million."

"I wouldn't even give you money."

Mark: Why won't you play on Vincent's team, Danny?

"He's black. That's why."

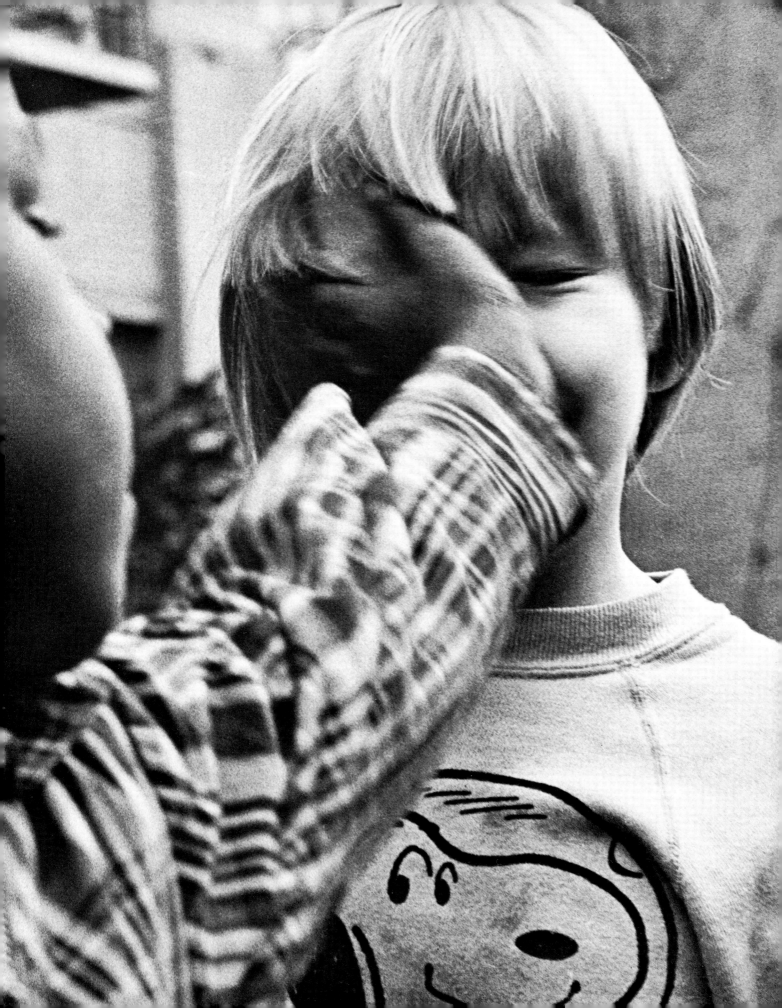

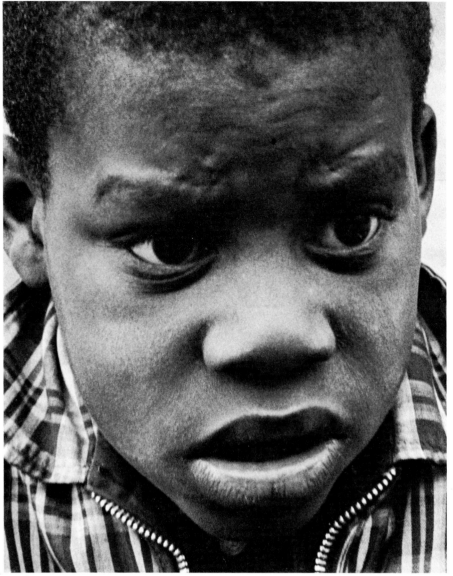

"Why'd you do that, Danny? I don't like that.
I don't like the way you said that."

"You had no right to hit me."

"You don't have no right to say what you said."

"It's just that you're all good players. You're all good players.
I'm a bum."

"I ain't good. Look at all the strikes I made.
You think I'm good, right?"

"You make me cry, and I got eye trouble.
You're making fun of me.
You think it's funny."

"I don't think it's funny."

"Yeah, you do."

Vincent: What would you do if someone called you that?

Mark: It doesn't matter what color you are.
He could play.

Vincent: I wish you were colored green or pink. . . .
You are green . . . green slime.
If I said to you. "I don't want to play with
you because you're black," what would you do?

Ivan: I'd hit you.

Vincent: I already did it. I didn't want to hit Danny.
But I didn't like it when he said that to me.
Danny got hurt though.

"I'm sorry for when I called you black, Vincent."

"What'd you say?"

"I'm sorry for when I called you black."

"You said you didn't want to play. But I don't want to start that again."

"I'm sorry. I'm just a bum player."

"You were just mad at me.
You're . . . it starts with j and ends with s: jealous."

"Jealous? You can run faster."

"That don't mean nothing. You were just mad at me. That's all."

"When we're together, it's all right. That's all."